Brilliant Brain
Banishes Boredom

Ellen Arnold

Illustrations by Deborah Farber

Zephyr
Press ®
REACHING THEIR HIGHEST POTENTIAL
Tucson, Arizona

Acknowledgments

—To Michaela, whose life need never be boring—

Creating books takes work. But when you have a great team, the process can be joyful. Deborah Farber's picture-smart part helped develop my ideas into a wonderful visual presence. Marti Arnold's word- and number-smart parts were an invaluable asset in helping me be clear, concise, and consistent. Without their patience, ideas, and support, this project would still be in my mind rather than in your hands.

Brilliant Brain Banishes Boredom

Grades K–4

© 2000 by Ellen Arnold.

Printed in the United States of America

ISBN 1-56976-115-9

Editor: Bonnie Lewis
Design & Production: Daniel Miedaner
Cover Design: Daniel Miedaner
Illustrations: Deborah Farber

Published by
Zephyr Press
P.O. Box 66006
Tucson, Arizona 87528-6006
http://zephyrpress.com
http://giftsforteachers.com

Library in Congress Cataloging-in-Publication Data

Arnold, Ellen, 1944-
     Brilliant Brain banishes boredom / by Ellen Arnold ; illustrated by Deborah Farber.
          p. cm
     ISBN 1-56976-115-9 (alk.)
     1. Attention-deficit disordered children—Education—Juvenile literature. 2. Attention-deficit hyperactivity disorder—Juvenile literature. [1. Attention-deficit hyperactivity disorder.] 1. Farber, Deborah, ill. II. Title.

LC4713.2 .A78 2000
371.93—dc21   00-030383

Brilliant Brain Banishes Boredom

A Note to Teachers and Parents:

This book is dedicated to the bright students with ADHD—who are gifted in making many connections, whose brains are rich in associations and creative thinking, but whose classroom experiences may often be distressing (and their teachers' experience as well). I hope Brilliant can help them develop strategies to be more successful in school. *MI Strategies for Kids,* a teacher/parent manual, describes a lesson plan that will help make this book a most useful tool for the learner.

Brilliant Brain's mind works in many ways. He likes to think. His mind is active, going from one thing to another. It is exciting to think about all the things he can think about. Sometimes, Brilliant thinks about many things at once. Sometimes his brain races really fast. It often thinks at a different speed than the people around him. Brilliant is rarely bored when he can let his mind "go with the flow." But when others expect his thinking to stay within a specific area, he finds himself easily bored.

Brilliant was trying to pay attention to his teacher's directions. She said they were starting a new unit on the planets and the stars. She started talking about all the things they would learn. Brilliant thought of how the planets reminded him of balls. All of a sudden, Brilliant's brain was on the baseball field, replaying yesterday's exciting game. He was cheering while his sister, Magnificent Mind, rounded the bases to win the game.

Teacher: *Brilliant! What are you doing? Weren't you paying attention?*

BB: What? Oh, uh, huh?

Brilliant realized he was still in class and not on the baseball field.

Teacher: *Brilliant, this is happening far too often. I think you should bring your parents to school tomorrow for a conference, so we can talk about how often you are* **not** *paying attention. This is a major problem!*

Brilliant slumped in his chair. He didn't mean to relive the baseball game. He didn't want his teacher or his parents to be mad at him. He was just so bored. The work was certainly

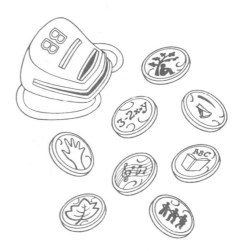

easy enough. It just didn't capture his attention. When he felt bored, his mind just got on a magic carpet and took him someplace more interesting. He didn't want to get into trouble. He just didn't have any idea what to do about his brain.

A fter school, Brilliant searched in his room for his strategy bank. Once he found it, he went through all the strategies he had inside. There were strategies for spelling and strategies for listening and strategies for reading, but he couldn't find any strategies for not being bored. He decided to visit the Smart Parts, who lived on, around, and through Intelligence Avenue, to see if they had any more strategies he could try.

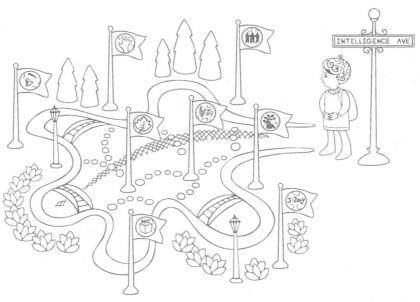

H e marched down the Avenue and came to a rest area, where he heard Music Smart practicing. He explained his problem using rhyme because he knew that Music Smart would understand him better if he spoke in a song or with a beat.

BB: Music Smart, can you help me?
In school I need a remedy
'Cause my brain wanders all the time.
When I'm not bored, I do just fine.
My teacher thinks I do not care;
Any strategies you can share?

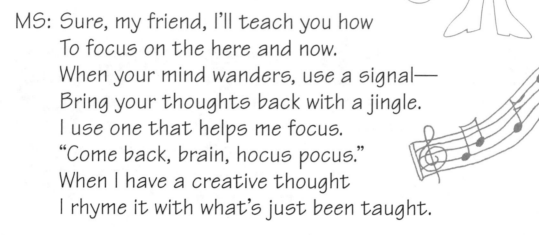

MS: Sure, my friend, I'll teach you how
To focus on the here and now.
When your mind wanders, use a signal—
Bring your thoughts back with a jingle.
I use one that helps me focus.
"Come back, brain, hocus pocus."
When I have a creative thought
I rhyme it with what's just been taught.

*B*rilliant thought about the unit they were studying in school. The teacher said they were going to learn about astronomy, the planets, and stars. Brilliant started to hum. It was a song he had learned a long time ago.

BB: Twinkle, twinkle, little star
How I wonder . . .

*B*ut pretty soon his mind wandered away from the original song and he was making up new words. Each thought led to another, and pretty soon he was having a great time thinking.

BB: Twinkle, twinkle, little star,
Are you made of marshmallow tar?
Like a diamond in the sky
You flash and shine, I wonder why.

6

MS: Brilliant, you make great connections
    Just jot them down for more reflection.
    Create some sounds to let you know
    Your brain is focused on this show.
    Then you'll get the information
    Because your brain paid close attention.

BB: But I cannot stop the flow
    Of ideas or things I want to know.
    My thoughts follow on their own track
    I don't know how to bring them back.

MS: You can learn to control your mind.
    Put your ideas where they're easy to find.
    Use sticky notes or lists in order,
    Songs, charts, or a tape recorder.
    Once you've tucked your idea away
    Come back to the topic of today.

BB: When I hear music I often tap
    My teacher says, "Hands in your lap."
    If music is playing in my head
    I might miss what the teacher said.

MS: Again, my friend, slow down your brain,
    Make connections to ease the strain.
    Remember key words the teachers use,
    Record them any way you choose.
    Later, sort them and reflect
    And let your brain play and connect.

BB: Is this the strategy that works for you?
    Do you get bored in classrooms too?

MS: My mind connects to things I know
    I watch the pace, not fast or slow.
    I use "hocus pocus" and in a wink
    My attention is on what I need to think!"

BB: I need to practice this I think,
    But it should keep my brain in sync.
    You make learning so much fun
    But now I really have to run.

Think of a way you can KNOW if your brain has wandered away.

Hocus Pocus, Brain Focus

*B*rilliant continued wandering down Intelligence Avenue until he saw Picture Smart taking pictures of the beautiful scenery.

BB: Picture Smart, you are always so good at seeing the right thing. I need a vision. Sometimes in school I get bored and my mind just wanders. Can you help me banish boredom?

PS: I can see myself when I was in school. I had the same problem. But I learned some wonderful strategies that I can show you.

BB: I'd love to see them.

PS: You know how much I like to take pictures and make movies?

BB: Yes.

PS: Well, I keep my video camera going all the time. No matter what I am doing, I think about how to make a video of it. When I am reading, I think about what the characters and the setting look like. Sometimes I make my movie into a cartoon. Sometimes it is one picture with lots of detail. Sometimes I make it silly. But I always leave my creativity on so that I can connect my fun pictures to the information I am learning. If I turn my camera off, my mind wanders, too. As long as I leave my camera on, I can stay focused.

BB: I can picture that.

*B*rilliant turned on the camera inside his brain. He saw his teacher in front of the class.

9

BB: I see my teacher drawing the planets but they don't look very interesting. They look just like bouncing balls.

PS: Why don't you paint them? Think about colors or shapes that remind you of what they are like.

BB: Well, Mercury is little. I can paint it bright red, like a tiny tomato.

PS: That's a great start, Brilliant. Keep painting.

BB: Venus could be light yellow. It reminds me of one of my mother's favorite necklaces, made of round shiny pearls.

PS: You've got the picture, Brilliant.

BB: The earth has swirls of blue and green and white, like a fancy marble. Mars is a great big red rubber ball like the one we bounce during gym class. Jupiter is really big, I can add a great big smiley face in the middle. Saturn has rings that I can paint like whirling hula hoops. Uranus looks flat. I'll make it into a light blue Frisbee. And Pluto is shiny, so I'll make it look like a big round ball of ice. Hey, Picture Smart, this is fun.

PS: See, Brilliant, when you picture things and make them fun, your boredom goes away.

BB: And I can make them into anything I want. I think the pictures will help me remember the planets, too.

PS: That's right, Brilliant. And you never have to worry about being bored when you carry your camera and paintbrushes in your head.

BB: Thanks, Picture Smart. I'll put the "Paint Pictures" strategy into my strategy bank. Brilliant ran down Intelligence Avenue, across the park, and over a bridge to collect some more strategies. Body Smart was working out.

Paint Pictures

BB

What pictures do you see in your head?

BB: Body Smart, do you have some strategies you use as tools to keep from being bored? I get into trouble in school because I get bored and my mind wanders.

BS: I used to have that problem, but I have learned what to do about it. I know I have to be moving all the time not to get bored.

BB: Yes, but moving gets me into trouble. The teacher says I am bothering other kids.

BS: Well, your brain needs you to move, to stay alert. People move all the time. Watch others closely and see how often they move. I learned to move so no one notices.

BB: How am I going to do that?

BS: I'll walk you through it. Think about something you were supposed to do in class today.

Make a list of movements that others think of as legal (examples: blink eyes, twirl hair, switch weight from one side to the other).

Brilliant told Body Smart about what happened this morning. His teacher was reading a story about living on the moon. Brilliant was supposed to pay attention so he could answer the questions at the end. But the story seemed boring. Pretty soon his mind wandered away. Before he knew it, he wasn't paying attention at all, and he didn't know what the story was about.

BS: What you need to do, Brilliant, is connect your movement to the story. When the teacher starts to read or talk or explain something, you need to use movement as a hook for your attention. If I were in your place this morning, I would think about what it would be like to be on the moon. How fast could I run? What games could I play? What tools would work best?

What movements would you connect to being in a space-ship?

U.S.S. BRILLIANT

Brilliant thought about that. He imagined being on a rocket ship at lift off. He could feel himself being pushed back against the seat. Once he got to the moon, what would it be like to walk around? Would he float? How far could he kick a soccer ball? As he tried to feel what his body would be like on the moon, he lost all track of time. He wasn't bored at all. This was fun.

*B*ody Smart did 100 sit ups and stacked a pile of wood while he waited for Brilliant to finish thinking.

BS: Brilliant, are you on the right track?

BB: Huh? What? Oh, Body Smart. I was having such a good time. I felt like I had just traveled all the way to the moon. I was floating and playing soccer—it felt like I was really there.

BS: Were you bored?

BB: Bored. No way. It was fun.

BS: Do you know what you did?

BB: Well, I guess I used my Body Smart Part—I moved and connected the movement to what I was supposed to learn. Is this the "Move to Connect" strategy?

BS: You've got it!

BB: I think moving will help me remember—I don't seem to be bored when I am moving. I just need to learn to move so it doesn't bother anyone else. Did I move a lot just now?

BS: Not too much. I could see you tightening and loosening your muscles but you weren't moving a whole lot. With practice, you can learn to move your muscles without anyone else even knowing. I do it all the time and no one can even tell. I have even learned to run a race without getting out of my chair.

BB: How do you do that?

BS: I just tighten and loosen my leg muscles, one after the other, just as I would if I were running a race. My feet don't move, but my legs get tired because I really do work my muscles. And I pay attention the best when I am running. Then I pretend I'm running to the place I'm supposed to be thinking about.

BB: Thanks, Body Smart. I think the "Move to Connect" strategy will work for me.

*B*rilliant added this to his strategy bank, and then went in search of other Smart Parts so he could collect more strategies. Brilliant wandered along Intelligence Avenue until he spotted Self Smart staring up at the sky.

BB: Self Smart, can you think about how to help me not be bored? Today in school we started to study the sky and the planets, and I got bored and my mind wandered to the baseball game yesterday, and then I got into trouble. I really want to learn, Self Smart, but I can't feel excited just by the words the teacher says. I don't want to be a failure. Can you think of something I can do?

SS: Sure. I am never bored, Brilliant. I can teach you how to do what I do. I think and think. Why is the sky blue?

BB: Just because it is, I guess. But what does that have to do with being bored?

SS: Just think about it. Keep thinking. Ask yourself questions like "Why?" and "How?" Make the questions big ones, not just fact ones. Make up questions that make you really think.

*S*o Brilliant thought about why the sky was blue. Why is it deep blue on some days and a different blue on other days? How come sometimes it is white? How does it turn gray? Sometimes it is black. How does that happen? Once he saw a beautiful reddish orange circle in the sky. And he even saw a brightly colored rainbow once. Why do people say that the sky is blue? Lots of times it isn't blue. What really does cause all those other colors? He thought about this for a long time.

SS: Brilliant, are you still there?

BB: Oh, hi, Self Smart. I have been thinking about the sky and colors. Do the colors have something to do with the light? I mean there are more colors when the sun is out than at nighttime. But that doesn't answer how it changes. I'd like to learn more about that.

SS: I don't think you were bored, were you?

BB: No way, I was really into thinking. I have lots of questions and ideas.

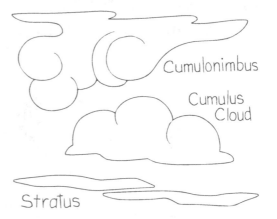

SS: Were your thoughts connected to the topic?

BB: I think so. I was thinking about the sky and colors.

SS: So what strategy did you use?

BB: The "Question It" strategy!

SS: Yes. And I think you could become really good at using it, if you practiced.

BB: **But won't I get lost in my thinking and forget what I am supposed to be learning?**

How do you feel when you get bored?

SS: Maybe, so you need to test yourself and ask yourself whether your thoughts are on target.

BB: **Can I do that myself? Usually the teacher or my mom tests me.**

SS: You don't need to wait for the teacher. You can test yourself. That is also a fun way to keep from being bored. Just reflect to yourself, "Is my current thinking related to the topic?"

BB: **Thanks for the "Question It" strategy, Self Smart. I think I could get really good at this.**

So Brilliant went off to think some more about the "Question It" strategy.

WS: Inform, convey, declare, narrate, recount . . .

BB: **Word Smart. Hi. What do you say?**

WS: I'm learning more words.

BB: **Don't you ever get tired of words? Grownups talk a lot. And sometimes the words don't seem to mean anything. Sometimes when people use lots of words I get bored, and then I can't pay attention anymore. Did that ever happen to you?**

WS: Sure. But I have a great strategy for that. Words are fascinating. Whenever I am learning something new, I think about the letters and the word parts. I play with the words and make new words, and that helps me learn them. It's fun to think about words.

BB: **I don't know if I can do that, Word Smart. I'm not very good with words.**

WS: Sure you are. You just don't know you are. Let's take your own name. Do you know the letters?

BB: **Yes.**

WS: See how many words you can make with the letters of your name.

BRILLIANT

ran	bill	till	lab	blab
rain	bran	Tall	lair	tar
rant	brain	tail	lint	air
rail	ball	trail	lit	ail
rat	ban	train	liar	bat
rib	bar	tan	nab	bail
a	barn	tin	nail	it
at	brat	tab	nil	I'll
ant	bib	trial	ill	all
art	bit	bin	in	Libra

WS: Let's see, *Brilliant.* Well, there was *ill,* but I don't want to think about being sick. And here is *ant.* Hum. Any more words? Well, if I move the letters around a little, I can make some more. *bill ran tan lit lamb brain rib alibi*

BB: This is fun. But am I learning anything when I am playing with words? I am supposed to be learning about the planets and the stars.

WS: Sure you are. Your brain is hungry for connections when you are bored. It needs more to think about. So take the words and play with them. That way the neurons in your head are making lots of connections. The more connections you make, the better the words will stick. Why not let words help you learn the names of planets? Take the first letter of the names of all the planets. Then make up a sentence with new words but using the same first letter.

BB: **Mercury, Venus, Earth, Mars, Jupiter, Saturn, Neptune, Uranus, Pluto...What about "My Very Eager Mother Jumps and Sings, but Never Under Pressure."**

WS: Cool. Do you think you will remember that?

BB: **Sure. It is fun to make up my own sentences. It is like a game.**

WS: That's how I feel, Brilliant. I just took the first letters of each of the planets, and I made a silly word *vumm* pens. I can imagine that these pens can write on any planet, regardless whether there is gravity or not. They won't spill or stain, and they always write. They are a *joy* (because I left out Jupiter).

BB: **Wow. You are really good at this "Make Up a Word or Sentence" strategy, Word Smart. By having this much fun playing with the words, I won't have to study.**

WS: That's right, Brilliant. When you play with words and letters, and make up sentences or stories, it makes it much easier to remember. You learn it so well when you first learn it that you don't have to study it later.

Try to write your name using letters from the planets' names. How many planets' names did you have to use?

Make Up a Word or Sentence

BB: Thank you, Word Smart, for this fun strategy. I'll put it in my strategy bank and be on my way. I want to get all the way around Intelligence Avenue in my search for strategies.

*S*o Brilliant hiked down the path, counting the stepping stones, when he spotted Number Smart using a calculator.

BB: Number Smart, I have a big problem. My teacher has been counting all the times I am not paying attention, and she says it is way too many—at least ten times a day. I need a plan. Do you have a formula that will solve my problem?

NS: Is there any pattern to when you get bored? Is it at a certain time of the day?

BB: Gee, I never thought about any of those things. Why would they be important?

NS: Patterns. If you can figure out a pattern, you can better figure out the answer. I can be more focused the first time my hands go around each day than I am the second time. That's a pattern.

BB: You mean, in the morning instead of the afternoon?

NS: Exactly. And my mind wanders the most when I am doing geometry problems, but I never get bored when I am doing multiplication or timelines. I love those.

BB: You get bored with some kinds of math problems? I thought you loved anything to do with math.

NS: I do, but some problems interest me more, and when I am more interested, I can pay attention longer and better. I figure out the pattern, so I know when I need to plan to use more strategies in order to be focused.

BB: I don't know of any pattern. I guess I'll have to think about that some more.

NS: Well, you can spend some time with Self Smart to think and reflect about your patterns, but in the meantime, you could do an experiment to gather some data. Tomorrow, in school, do a timeline and mark down the number of times you catch yourself not paying attention during the day. If you do that for a couple of days, you can bring the data back here, and I'll be glad to help you analyze it. Don't forget to give yourself a point for every time you *are* paying attention.

BB: **Data? Formulas? Numbers? I like doing charts. Do you think I can collect data and make charts for the unit we are doing on the planets?**

NS: Sure, graphs and charts are wonderful ways to organize any kind of information. I'll bet you could make up a chart yourself. Include all the facts you need to learn and this will help you stay focused on the important points. Scientists who study the planets use charts all the time.

BB: **They do? Well, I guess my chart could have the names of the planets and maybe their size, how far they are from the sun, or the number of moons. I could include all kinds of things.**

Name of PLANET	Size	Distance from Sun	Rotation Time	# of Moons	Temp.	Other
Mars						
Venus						
Earth						

NS: That's right. So what do you think of the "Chart It" strategy? Will it help you?

BB: I like it, and I think it will keep me from getting bored. I'll definitely put this strategy in my strategy bank. Thank you, Number Smart.

When your brain gets bored, do you escape to:
- something in the past?
- something in the future?

What would happen if you focused on the moment instead?

*B*rilliant trekked around the park on Intelligence Avenue, thinking about all the things to put in his chart. He saw Nature Smart feeding the birds.

BB: Nature Smart, I am learning about stars and planets in school, and my mind keeps wandering. What do you do when you are learning so that you don't get bored?

NS: I use my "Find the Contribution" strategy. When I am learning something new about the world, I think about what this thing contributes to our lives. Well, think about the stars. What do the stars contribute to your life?

BB: Nothing. They don't talk, and they don't sing, and they don't play soccer.

NS: You mean you have never talked with a star?

BB: No way!

NS: Hmm. Haven't you ever wished upon a star?

BB: Sure, "Star light, star bright, bring me the wish I wish tonight."

NS: And have you ever been outside at night and looked at the stars?

BB: Yes, last summer when we went camping. Magnificent and I stayed up really late and just looked at all the different patterns of the stars. They were so bright and beautiful. We could even see in the dark, because of the light of the stars.

NS: Well, so far you have given me a few contributions. Something to wish on, beautiful patterns and light. Anything else?

BB: Well, looking at the stars gave me a feeling of how small I am and how I lucky I am.

NS: Aha, so the stars also changed your feelings!

BB: I see what you mean, Nature Smart. I guess I was just taking the stars for granted and not really thinking about how they affected me.

NS: Unfortunately, many people take nature for granted, Brilliant. Part of my job is to remind people about the importance of nature and how we need to make sure we don't destroy it.

How have stars contributed to your life?

BB: But how will this help keep me from being bored?

NS: If you are learning something new, keep asking yourself what this "thing" does for the world . . . how would my life be different if it didn't exist?

BB: That sounds like a fun thing to think about. I could get into that.

NS: Great. So do you want to put the "Find the Contribution" strategy in your strategy bank?

BB: I sure do. Thanks, Nature Smart, for helping me understand this strategy. I won't take the stars for granted anymore.

Find the Contribution Strategy

*B*rilliant was talking to himself as he meandered over a bridge and down a stone path. He overheard People Smart talking to some friends.

27

PS: Brilliant! We can always make time for you, my friend. How are you?

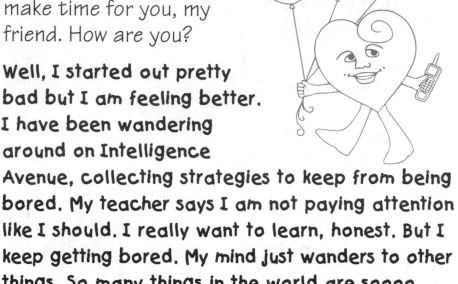

BB: Well, I started out pretty bad but I am feeling better. I have been wandering around on Intelligence Avenue, collecting strategies to keep from being bored. My teacher says I am not paying attention like I should. I really want to learn, honest. But I keep getting bored. My mind just wanders to other things. So many things in the world are soooo interesting. But my teacher wants me to learn all about the planets and stars. It was boring to me! So I have been collecting strategies from the Smart Parts.

PS: What have you learned so far?

BB: I'll show you all the new strategies I have put in my strategy bank.

BB: Here is the "Hocus Pocus, Brain Focus" strategy that I got from Music Smart. It will help me signal my brain to come back to what I am supposed to be thinking about.

BB: And here is my "Paint Pictures" strategy that I got from Picture Smart. By using the camera and paintbrush in my brain I can make information colorful. If I really think about the colors and what they mean, I won't be bored.

BB: The "Move to Connect" strategy, of course, came from Body Smart. It keeps me on track by letting me move in ways that make the learning real for me but don't bother anyone else.

BB: Then I got the "Question It" strategy from Self Smart. If I come up with my own questions about the information, like giving myself a test, then I can be thinking about the new information and keeping my mind interested at the same time.

BB: The "Make Up a Word or Sentence" strategy came from Word Smart. I can make up new words or sentences from the letters of the words I need. This will keep my brain busy and still help me focus on what is important.

BB: Number Smart gave me the "Chart It" strategy. I can make a chart that will help me think and keep my brain involved.

BB: This last strategy is from Nature Smart. It is the "Find the Contribution" strategy. When I use this strategy, I have to think about how my life would be different if the thing I am studying didn't exist.

BB: So I have learned a lot of great strategies today. Do you have any more to share with me, to keep myself from being bored?

PS: We used to get bored too. But you know how much we like people and being friends. Well, we learned to make friends with the information.

BB: I never heard of that before.

PS: When you are learning something, you want to treat the information like you would if it were a new student in class whom you wanted to befriend. What would you do if a family named "The Planets" moved next door to you?

BB: I guess I'd ask them over to play. I'd find out what they were like and what they liked to do. I'd want to know where they moved from and how old they are. You know, just stuff so I could understand them better.

PS: So do the same thing with the planets in the sky. Use the same questions and see what happens.

BB: Hmm. What are they like? What do they do? Where did they come from? How old are they? How did they get here? I guess these questions work for the planets as well as for people.

PS: Yes. And when you use the "Make Friends with the Information" strategy, learning no longer seems boring.

BB: Cool, People Smart. I'd like to add this to my strategy bank. Thanks.

*B*rilliant went back to his house on Intelligence Avenue to sort all his new strategies. Now that he had so many strategies to choose from, he could take control of his brain so it didn't wander when it was supposed to be doing something else.

Which of Brilliant's new strategies do you want to try?

Do you have a strategy that has worked for you when you get bored?

*R*emember, you can banish boredom by using your smart parts. Just turn on your smart parts, including your radio, your camera, your actions, asking yourself questions, your words, your charts, your understanding of nature, and your knowledge of people—then you won't be bored. You'll be a smart, strategic learner, just like Brilliant.

Option A   Option B